PRAISE FOR JACQUELINE PIRTLE

"Jacqueline takes you always directly to what you are ready to see or experience."

— LONGTIME CLIENT AND READER

"It is liberating to face your own blocks and to be finally free of the weight that they have caused for many years. And while for me the changes I'm experiencing are noticeable and real, I still feel like myself. Just a more sure self."

— LONGTIME CLIENT AND READER

"Jacqueline makes me BELIEVE I can be and live a joyful and magical existence every new day of my life!"

— LONGTIME CLIENT AND READER

JACQUELINE PIRTLE

High for Life

The best case scenario!

A 90 day journal

THE EXTENDED EDITION

COPYRIGHT

Copyright © 2021 Jacqueline Pirtle
www.FreakyHealer.com

All rights reserved. No part of this book may be reproduced or transmitted in any form or by any means, electronic or mechanical, including photocopying, recording, or by any information storage and retrieval system without the written permission of the publisher, except where permitted by law.

ISBN-13: 978-1-955059-17-6

Publisher: Freaky Healer

Editor-in-chief: Zoe Pirtle
All-round Support: Mitch Pirtle

Book cover design by Kingwood Creations kingwoodcreations.com

Author photo courtesy of Lionel Madiou madious.com

I want to let you know that all my books and holistic practitioner work together are a wholesome system, supporting you to live a more conscious, mindful, and happier life.

However, I made it so you can receive the benefit of living more joyously solely by working through this terrific journal book, while also experiencing the full satisfaction in continuing on to the next journal of this series—not to mention the rock solid tools you get by reading any of my other books or adding in my podcast *The Daily Freak*. Either way, I know you'll love my inspirational teachings.

Find out more at:
www.freakyhealer.com
Amazon Author Page
The Daily Freak Podcast

Before you dive in, I want to thank you for hopping on the magic train with me! I truly hope you enjoy *High for Life* as much as I loved writing it, and if you do, it would be wonderful if you could take a short minute and leave a review on Amazon.com and Goodreads.com as soon as you can.

Your kind feedback helps other readers find my books more easily, and be happy faster. Consider it a happy deed for the world.

Thank you!

ACKNOWLEDGMENTS

Let's be honest here… I have a dream team!

I could not have finished this book without the help of talented, creative, high-for-life, and phenomenal professionals.

From the bottom of my heart, I want to thank Zoe Pirtle for her editorial mastery; Mitch Pirtle for his all-round support; kingwoodcreations.com for their fun and polished book cover design; and madiouART.com for an amazing photo shoot.

I'd also like to extend a huge "Thank You!" to all fans of my work and books—I created this beautiful journal series for you.

Life is spectacular with you on my side!

What's your happy place?
Go there, stay there, and never leave!

DEDICATION

*I dedicate this journal to all those that think that being **high-for-life** is not in the cards, and challenge them to make it **BE** their path!*

INTRODUCTION

Phenomenal *high-for-lifer*,

How cool is it that our paths are crossing—and even better, that together we will create well-feeling, love, happiness, and bliss while thriving to live a life that's worth loving?

High for Life is something I incorporate and talk about in all areas of my work—now, I have even created a journal about it, so let me explain.

High-for-life is a state of being where you are aligned with your true you, your well-feeling, and your happiness—whatever that might be and no matter the circumstances, because sometimes being angry or sad is exactly that. Nothing can inspire you to be anyone or anything else than yourself when you are in your high-for-life frequency. It is a state of constant change that is aligned with the flow of life; and a deeply, securely, rooted-as-yourself way of being and living.

Everything is energy - you, me, this journal, and all of life - and it's all *ONE* and the same: Energy! It's also all connected and shared at all times—meaning that you, living through these high-for-life ways that you are creating in this journal, will spread to

INTRODUCTION

everything and everyone lifting the whole world into a higher state, or at least as high as they want to go with you.

As these energies, everything and everyone vibrates in different frequencies—some are higher, like being in wonder about life, while others are lower, like not loving your life. Every scenario always has a high-for-life version as well as a low-for-life version—or one lower than the highest possibility. Embracing all of them is incredibly powerful; however, things get super exciting when you consciously choose which way you want life to be and how you want to feel.

High for Life helps you to see all of the different scenarios that are possible, while dreaming up and feeling your own personal high-for-life preferences for everything at anytime—pushing you to go for the best of the best at all times. There, an ocean of opportunities will catch hold of you, inviting you to latch on. Just think of that incredible match-up and shift into the higher frequency of bliss, by being *ONE* with the excitement of these manifestations.

A high-for-life way of living gives your best version of you the stage and momentum—all while changing at a constant and vivid speed and in the flow with how life naturally happens.

Journaling through this 90 day extended edition of ***High for Life*** brings huge uplifts into the equation so you can experience life like you never have before, craft a time beyond your expectations, and love what you live—to the extent of becoming a master in living consciously and mindfully, feeling phenomenal while manifesting the best of the best. It's a change that is forever!

As a side note, there are a couple of bonus days at the end in case you ever find the need to do two in a day, or so you can keep working while you wait for the next journal in this series to arrive. I also left you a few blank **high-for-life** pages to journal about deepening your ways of being alive.

Enough chit-chat, I know you are ready—so grab your pen

and have incredible fun with catching more life than you have ever caught, in your new crazy ways.

Happiest,
 Jacqueline

 Day 1

IMAGINE yourself standing at the top of a cliff! Don't worry nothing horrible is going to happen, just a little craziness for starters. So on that cliff: you feel powerful and are with clear focus, a still mind, and a neutral heart—you ARE! With excitement you peek up to see the beautiful sky and squint down to see Mother Earth while breathing into these beautiful sights. You are given two choices that are representing two different ways of living. One is to be able to fly freely, lift up weightlessly, and go wherever whenever you want to. It's a chance at being in charge, claiming your birth right to choose, and flying higher than you have ever flown—a scenario of having freedom while fully standing in your power. The other option is to fall freely and land safely wherever the wind blows you—offering freedom but giving up your birthright to choose and fly high. Both possibilities are an essence of being free but number one is a high-for-life experience, whereas the other is of limited value. Please tell me you want to fly! Then, without taking off yet, bathe in your exciting choice and journal about how this feels all while holding your horses until you take off tomorrow.

_____
_____
_____
_____
_____
_____
_____

High for Life - The best case scenario!

ay 2

TODAY'S THE DAY! Are you ready to fly? Go on, jump! Trust that you can fly, and rise freely into the height of a life that's perfect for you. Claim your birthright to choose for yourself and step into your power of being you. How does that best case scenario feel? What do you see and hear all the way up here? What inspirations are coming in for you? Is your heart exploding with joy, bliss, and aliveness? Are you ready to scream from the top of your lungs, "I AM alive, I AM living, I AM high-for-life"? Waste not a single minute, write about the flight to your best case scenario!

High for Life - The best case scenario!

 ay 3

YESTERDAY WE COVERED YOUR BIRTHRIGHT. Today, we talk about your birth-suit! Why? Because high-for-life resembles your birth-suit perfectly, since you came here to align with who you really are—which at the core is to BE and live highly. So when you feel happy, know that it's your perfect style. When you are laughing, you are in your fitting garment. When you are shedding a good-feeling tear, you're wearing your gorgeous outfit of emotions. When you feel good - no matter the *what* and *why* - you are dressed top notch as YOU because, after all, you are a professional high-for-lifer and it suits you! What's the visual? Write, journaler, write!

High for Life - The best case scenario!

 ay 4

T<small>HE WORD</small> *high* comes with an energetic value of high, higher, and highest, and is in direct alignment with your inner you because your soul being is always guiding you to BE your highest self. *High* also includes an essence of better, more, elevated, uplifted, lighter, and purer.

Saying and thinking the word *high*, and feeling its energy, shifts you directly into a high-for-life frequency.

If you hear the word *high* it's natural to look upward, not down, meaning that through the action of looking up you immediately shift to BE upward—and into a higher frequency than before.

How will you consciously align with all the high-ness in life, and at the same time your highest you?

_____
_____
_____
_____
_____
_____
_____
_____
_____
_____
_____
_____
_____
_____

High for Life - The best case scenario!

 ay 5

THE WORD *for* is of utmost value when said, thought of, or felt, because it is saturated with positivity—freeing you from resistance, pressure, or any such exhausting patterns. Just think about it; even as an action it ultimately has winning energy attached—you push *for* something. You fight *for* one thing, you go *for* what's aligned with who you really are. *For* is powerful and magical all at the same time! How will you incorporate much more of that *for* you?

*** High for Life - The best case scenario!***

 ay 6

THE WORD *LIFE* is deeply meaningful in your physical department because it speaks of your truth that you are alive—all while letting you expand and calibrate energetically.

Sensing yourself into the essence of *life* means you shift into a frequency of possibilities, love, and excitement, while also into pain, sadness, and anger—because those too belong to being and living a beautiful life.

The act of living is one of change, action, and enjoyment—a beautiful and thrilling shift for you to latch onto and relish in without ever stopping.

How will you be more conscious of *life*—in words, in life itself, and in living your life? Is fully and vividly an option?

_____
_____
_____
_____
_____
_____
_____
_____
_____
_____
_____
_____
_____
_____
_____

High for Life - The best case scenario!

Day 7

THERE IS NO *ONE-SIZE-FITS-ALL*, ever! High-for-life is very individually felt because everyone is unique and here for their own special reason. Feeling highly also changes every split second, since life is ever-changing and so are you. For some right now feeling high-for-life is happiness, while for others, it is being deeply embedded in sadness; for some it's traveling around the world, and for others it's owning a house. But one thing is always the same and a given—high-for-life means that someone is feeling amazing, satisfied, or over the moon in their life. What is your own special dream right now, today, tomorrow, next week, or in the long run?

_____
_____
_____
_____
_____
_____
_____
_____
_____
_____
_____
_____
_____
_____
_____
_____

High for Life - The best case scenario!

 Day 8

High-for-life is a constant and vivid process that's needing your attention on all different levels of your whole being—physical and energetic. How will you make sure to feel physically wonderful? Is better and cleaner food an option, or perhaps a new way of moving? And energetically, how will you listen to your inner you and follow its wisdom—without rolling your eyes at the *sometimes* strange input?

High for Life - The best case scenario!

 Day 9

EVERYTHING IN LIFE has a high end and a low end - plus of course all the different heights in between - giving you endless choices in how you want to experience something or someone. High-for-life means that you align with the best case scenario! What in your world right now do you not love as is? List some of these offenders—realize that the way you perceive them is of a lower value. What would a higher - or the highest - frequency of these happenings look like? How do you feel in those higher ways? Remember; you can fly, you can rise, it's your birthright to choose, and you have the power to BE you.

___
___
___
___
___
___
___
___
___
___
___
___
___
___
___
___
___

High for Life - The best case scenario!

Day 10

A HIGH-FOR-LIFE WAY of living involves your action of actively doing something—like taking off on a spaceship to see limitlessness, parachute jumping to feel the buzz, taking a cold shower to be tough, or being silly to feel like a child again. But it can also be achieved by your powerful ability to imagine, visualize, or feel yourself into a great state. For example; if you are sitting in a boring meeting, start imagining yourself at the beach while feeling the sand between your toes. Voila, your high-for-life is created! What fabulousness do you have up your sleeve—to go from blah to *vive la vie?*

_____
_____
_____
_____
_____
_____
_____
_____
_____
_____
_____
_____
_____
_____
_____
_____

High for Life - The best case scenario!

 ay 11

FOR BALANCE SAKE, *always* doing something, being active, moving, being out and about, or experiencing out-of-this world cool stuff does not guarantee that you are always feeling high-for-life. Many times it is actually achieved by aligning with yourself in stillness or meditation while doing nothing, being bored, or spending time alone in nature. How can you pay more attention to what feeling good really means? How will you align with yourself more often?

___

High for Life - The best case scenario!

ay 12

IMAGINE you are hugging the sun while gushing gratitude and love towards it—as a thank you for all the high-for-life'ness it does for you. What would you say to the sun? How would you honor this bright light—is it by beaming yours strongly too, in order to support the sun to make the world even shinier? What else in your surroundings represents such high-for-life thankfulness? Is it a cookie—a smile, a rainbow, some $100 bills, or the sky? What will you say to those things, and how will you celebrate them? Keep choosing new items, people, and happenings—feel how you shift higher and higher while at it!

___

High for Life - The best case scenario!

 ay 13

WHAT ON OR inside your physical body represents high-for-life for you? Is it your heart and powerful love, a strain of hair that's playing with your face, your smile giving and catching happiness, a single cell that's keeping you alive, or your muscles that are tough as nails? Pick many, and list how your special parts make you feel while consciously sensing your shift into wellness. Then, think about what you could say to them—for instance, your heart. Would spilling some loving words or a love letter do? Be generous here. After all, we are talking about your glorious physicality!

High for Life - The best case scenario!

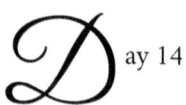 ay 14

Yesterday was all about the physical, today the energetic! What is the high-for-life value of your inner being—your soul, inner instinct, higher self, however you would like to call it? Is the deep wisdom, the always correct guidance, the constant knowing, or the unconditional and unlimited love that your energetic you has for you? Make your "I love my inner essence" list, and celebrate it to the moon and back—everyday!

High for Life - The best case scenario!

ay 15

THINK about the tasks in your everyday life, the ones that don't feel high-for-life. Make your "I don't like this!" list—it should be rebellious and fun. Now look at the other end of every task and find the high-for-life version—the *it's fine to do this*, and the *it's still a gift and a chance*. For instance, take cleaning the toilet; nobody really likes doing that, yet, at the other end of "nobody likes this" is the wonderful part of ending up with a clean bowl—and in case outsourcing feels highest, then that's the higher end of this task. There is a high-for-life version to everything and you can choose to find and focus on it—then sense yourself into the higher wellness of it.

High for Life - The best case scenario!

 Day 16

UNDERSTANDING AND ALSO ACCEPTING, respecting, appreciating, thanking, and loving the incredible fact that *everything* belongs to life is a high-for-life way of existing. The good, the bad, and the ugly, as we so beautifully say—it's all present and inclusive. Question is, how do you want to feel? What life do you want to live, and where will you put your focus—since all these controversies exist at all times?

High for Life - The best case scenario!

ay 17

You get to know yourself inside and out by feeling fully, and experiencing the vivid variety of your emotions—plus, embracing them as part of you belongs to a high-for-life way of living. Feeling freely means that you get really good at feeling yourself into alignment, and brings incredible wisdom about and for yourself, by giving you clues to when you are in the realm of flying high in your power—meaning, you can actually do something about it. Make your emotional list of *feeling good is flying high* and *not feeling good is flying low*, then come up with fitting solutions.

High for Life - The best case scenario!

ay 18

HIGH-FOR-LIFE DOES NOT ALWAYS mean happy. Any lower-frequency feeling starts out as feeling good at first—making it high-for-life at the beginning. Take anger, for example; in the first split second when you are angry it can feel good or at least better than not being angry—then after the initial up, you'll feel down, which is a clear sign that it's time for you to shift to a better feeling. Being angry is not a bad thing and neither is feeling crappy in your anger—however, staying unhappy could be. What feelings don't fit anymore, and what different ones do you desire—ready to shift?

High for Life - The best case scenario!

 ay 19

DREAMING up your perfect life is a high-for-life practice with enormous potency attached. It's a way to focus yourself energetically and then have it show up on your doorstep of physicality—that's the case for day dreaming, night dreaming, and all in-between dreams. So visualize, imagine, feel, and write your perfect story! This asks for you to not hold back, but to reach for the stars and way beyond for your wishes and desires. Go on dreamer, make it magical!

High for Life - The best case scenario!

 ay 20

HIGH-FOR-LIFE MEANS that you step into a pair of shoes even if they feel too big to fill—knowing that they only seem big because of your perception of being too little, not deserving, not capable, or being limited. Not because of the shoe being too big. What life puts in front of you and is inviting you to step into is *never* too big for you, instead, it always fits perfectly. "So tell me all about how you feel in these fitting shoes—and living your gigantic life!" says your journal.

High for Life - The best case scenario!

# Day 21

LIVING your life like it's a store in which you are invited to look around, shop for what you want, or order what interests you - while tasting a little here and there, and returning what's not right anymore - is a high-for-life way of existing. The best part is, it's the truth! What is your favorite shop—a clothing place, grocery store, travel agency, or farmers market? How do you behave when you are there, are you excited, feel eager, inspired, expecting, and abundant? Pretend that this store is your life and copy/paste your high-for-life ways into how you live your life.

___

High for Life - The best case scenario!

 Day 22

PAYING bills can seem like a downer activity: yet even that task has a high-for-life scenario by being an exchange, and every trade means there is a give and take—a balancing essence. But there is more! Paying bills makes the person on the receiving end happy —just like you felt when the goods were received. How will you change your attitude when paying your bills? How can you hold onto those uplifting thoughts, and pay through the energy of high-for-life?

High for Life - The best case scenario!

 ay 23

ALLOWING yourself to be new and fresh at every split second means you are high-for-life—besides going with the natural flow of how life rolls. How will you take this to heart? Is it by letting go of your jeans once you don't like them anymore, by finding different foods to taste deliciousness again, or by figuring out how to get in sync with yourself in a fresh new way? Same with your job, family, or loved ones—how can you be your always new you?

High for Life - The best case scenario!

 Day 24

TAKING life by the horns and riding *with* it all wildly and vividly is a high-for-life lifestyle! When was the last time you did that? What will it take for you to go jump into a freezing pool, write the book you always wanted to write, sing from the top of your lungs while not minding who's listening, love whoever you want to love, and feel like the luckiest person alive? Call me crazy—but only until you made your list, because after all, you are one of them too.

High for Life - The best case scenario!

# Day 25

FINDING the high-for-life in your pain is within reach! On the other end of pain there is always a golden opportunity to feel amazing - even when it's acute - by embracing your pain and accepting, respecting, appreciating, thanking, and loving this wonderful signal as the language of your body here to tell you more about yourself. Doing so shifts you into a resistance-free space where healing can take place. Where in your body are you hurting right now? What is your pain telling you, guiding you to do?

High for Life - The best case scenario!

Day 26

FOOD WANTS you to play with it - not fight - because having fun with food is part of being and living high-for-life! You are deeply invited to form a loving relationship with all that goes into your body—water included. So sense yourself into the energy of your food - energizing, clean, nourishing - and notice your automatic shift to the same frequency—making you energetically prepared to digest your food. Tap into how your food will make you feel once you've eaten it, and chit-chat with your food to form an open time of communication. Make your list of high-for-life foods that fill you with energy and aliveness, then keep coming back to add more favorites.

___

High for Life - The best case scenario!

Day 27

HIGH-FOR-LIFE MEANS that you find the most powerful and well-feeling way to deal with what's there for you right now while aligning with your strong you—your winner you. Sometimes that means asking for help and allowing that to be your strength—because taking care of your needs IS being strong. Other times, you find strength in doing it yourself even when it is hard—tapping into the power of "dealing with it." Make your list of happenings and strong-like-bull ways—then use the resulting clarity!

High for Life - The best case scenario!

 Day 28

It's good to be your own brave-heart and show up bolder than you were yesterday, or just a minute ago, because you constantly are expanding and calibrating into a higher, wider, and more powerful you. News flash—there is nothing wrong with you, your life, or with others if your *as-it-is* doesn't fit anymore. On the contrary; everything is right with everything, because you have outgrown the old. Bravo! What's getting on your nerves, feels too tight, or is not exciting anymore, and how would a better fitting scenario look like?

_____
_____
_____
_____
_____
_____
_____
_____
_____
_____
_____
_____
_____
_____
_____
_____

High for Life - The best case scenario!

 Day 29

FINDING your high-for-life in your lows is possible, because on the other end of all unwell-feeling emotions, there is always the gracious opportunity to feel wonderful even when in the abyss. Accepting, respecting, appreciating, thanking, loving all of you, and allowing how you feel to become your deepest truth barometer creates a space where whole-being wellness has a chance, because there, you get to know yourself really well. Where, with, what, whom, and how are you emotionally stretched? What is your mental state telling you? How can you love all of you?

___

High for Life - The best case scenario!

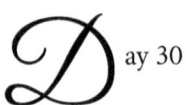

Day 30

Hurray! You are at the 30 day high-for-life mark! Are you skipping down your path of life? Did you color your hair orange yet, dressing like your own unique crazy you, wearing mismatched socks, or cooking breakfast for dinner and eating dessert as your entree? I hope to hear a "Yes, of course!" Otherwise, it's time to start skipping! What are your best case scenarios for living your crazy cool life?

High for Life - The best case scenario!

ay 31

CHIT-CHATTING with everything that is there for you is a crucial ingredient in living high-for-life. Why? Because of the wisdom it all holds. Ask a bug crawling up your leg, "What are you here for, what information do you have for me?" Or a yogurt that expired, "What do you represent for me?" Ask a feather flying in front of you, "What are you telling me?" What's grabbing your attention right now and what will you ask of it in order to squeeze the most out of life?

High for Life - The best case scenario!

 ay 32

Being stern at the right moment is in alignment with living a terrific life, but most of the time being alive does not ask you to be a properly serious person or experience things in such a severe energy. Where does it fit to be stern and where would a more lighthearted you be better? Your *being-stern-is-good* versus *let's-get-lighter* list please—because stern or not stern, that's the question!

High for Life - The best case scenario!

 ay 33

HIGH-FOR-LIFE IS LOVING YOUR HEART, and following it even if your mind - or other people - say otherwise. Your heart is the host of your inner being that always knows what's best for you, is made of unlimited energy, and needs to be the boss of your mind —like, has to run your mind. Don't get me wrong, your mind is a great tool, but it can lead you to the opposite of feeling good whereas your heart always guides you to what fits—that's why your mind following your heart will manifest what you love. Your marching orders are clear; focus on feeling good, then match your thoughts to that. So, what is your heart telling you?

_____
_____
_____
_____
_____
_____
_____
_____
_____
_____
_____
_____
_____
_____
_____
_____
_____

High for Life - The best case scenario!

 ay 34

SYNCHRONICITY IS the beautiful sign of being on your aligned high-for-life path! For example; you can't decide if you should or shouldn't go to an event, but then while walking through the mall you see the perfect outfit. Or like when you don't know if you should stay at a job, then they announce a big unfitting change that's coming up. Or when you are working on a project, and suddenly notice everything that's needed is showing up easy-peasy. What in your life are you questioning right now? Can you find synchronicity anywhere?

High for Life - The best case scenario!

 ay 35

INTENSITY BELONGS to a high-for-life experience and since there is never a ceiling to how much more intense things could be, how much more could you feel? What would you want to consciously feel more of? Of course, we are talking about the good feelings here—all of the others, tone them down. Take this clarity to an intense level and allow the guidance to receive *more* of what you like to flow—is it love, fun, or deliciousness?

High for Life - The best case scenario!

 ay 36

CLARITY IS A HIGH-FOR-LIFE ENTITY, because without it you don't know—meaning you are floating without being in control, and might even feel lost or weak. How will you go for clarity in your life more often? How will you stick with that created clarity and show yourself as such to your surroundings?

___

High for Life - The best case scenario!

# Day 37

HIGH-FOR-LIFE LIVING INCLUDES BEING in a space of relaxation where trusting in yourself and life is at a high point, and where you understand that as long as you are aligned with your inner being, you create an experience that is high-for-life. It also involves a deep knowing that you can shift at any time if something turns sour, and within seconds can live your high-for-life again—all while flowing with the truth that life and you are ever-changing and that constant lefts, rights, or ups and downs are OK! Are you that relaxed? How can - and will - you loosen up and trust more?

High for Life - The best case scenario!

 Day 38

Swimming is a great metaphor to realize the difference between upstream and downstream—one path is easy, while the other can be a fight. You guessed it—high-for-life is downstream! How does going with life feel for you? Where will you stop your *against* mentality, and instead, shift yourself to an aligned *with*? And for sake of clarity, when you see others swim against the stream, let them—because what looks like upstream to you might actually be their downstream, just not your downstream. They might also not know any better, and seeing you choose your downstream may be their hinting lightbulb. What are you waiting for? Swim journaler, swim!

_____
_____
_____
_____
_____
_____
_____
_____
_____
_____
_____
_____
_____
_____
_____

High for Life - The best case scenario!

ay 39

PLAYING around like a goofball is high-for-life—so much so that I don't even need to explain, let alone convince you. What, when, and whom is your playdate today? Goof-list please!

___

High for Life - The best case scenario!

 ay 40

MAKING mistakes can be the opposite scenario of feeling high-for-life. However, this is only the case if you think that mistakes are bad, wrong, or shouldn't be made—proving someone unworthy and incapable. I challenge you to turn all mistakes to be a higher essence, by allowing them to belong to a vivid life and be the creator for new solutions. Of course if they are life threatening do what you must do—but most of the time they are little, silly, and many turn out to be a gift in disguise. How will you giggle and laugh about mistakes more often—or at least breathe yourself into relaxation when they are happening?

High for Life - The best case scenario!

 Day 41

YESTERDAY, we got into the midst of mistakes, and hopefully you got some good humor going on by now. Today we go for solutions—high-for-life ones, that is! How can you roll with the opportunity for new ways to come in, which every mistake or problem naturally brings? What does a phenomenal solution look like—for anything? What does a great new way feel like; better than before, exciting, relieving, perfect?

_____
_____
_____
_____
_____
_____
_____
_____
_____
_____
_____
_____
_____
_____
_____
_____
_____
_____

High for Life - The best case scenario!

 ay 42

BEING full of yourself is high-for-life! Period! The unflattering meanings programmed into these words or actions are not true —you are not a bad person, selfish, self-obsessed, or caring only about yourself if you are full of yourself. Spiritually speaking, alignment is exactly that—a deep and centered connection with yourself, then showing up as such, and sharing and spreading the wonderfulness that is YOU with everything and everyone. What a deed! So, how full are you of yourself and how can you become fuller, or even over the brim, of yourself?

___

High for Life - The best case scenario!

 ay 43

MUTED IS on the opposite end of a high-for-life scenario—even when being still, and in meditation, your breath is always clearly vivid. Same goes for being meek or timid versus being full of yourself, showing up way too small versus being your gigantic energy, or being unsure versus undeniably knowing your truth. Too modest is always lower in frequency compared to a proud and bragging you because being too *less* doesn't let you show yourself, or anyone else, the way to live high-for-life; whereas being *too much* will let you move mountains—oh wait, too much of you doesn't even exist since there is never a ceiling to how much higher you can fly! Where are you *too less*, and how can you turn your volume up, up, and up-er?

___
___
___
___
___
___
___
___
___
___
___
___
___
___
___
___

High for Life - The best case scenario!

ay 44

KNOWING that you are a deserving being is one part of living your life in the highest form possible—showing up as a deserving essence is the other part, which completes your wholesomely deserving picture of yourself. As that complete deserving being you will be a force of kindness, maturity, and generosity—because what else could you be, knowing that there will always be more coming? Deserve, journaler, deserve! What will it be; a cookie, money, success, love, happiness, and a fabulous life?

High for Life - The best case scenario!

 ay 45

HIGH-FOR-LIFE MEANS that you taste life - yes, you can taste all of it, not just the food - fully and vividly! Close your eyes and relish in what a delicious life tastes like. List those uplifting words—is it sweet, delectable, divine, flavorful, appetizing, or spicy and hot? Voila, you have your marching orders! Keep journaling ahead, but do come back to add more and be amazed how many savor descriptors make up your dream life. Did you know that you are quite the gourmet lifer?

High for Life - The best case scenario!

 Day 46

IN A HIGH-FOR-LIFE EXPERIENCE, you can see life through colorful and creative lenses and beyond what your physical eyes can see. Close your eyes and witness what that might look like for you, write those exciting discoveries down. What colors do you prefer right now? Remember that they change all the time! What do they make you feel like; beachy, green, or red? What creativity gets you vividly thrilled; crafting, coloring, baking, or glueing? Mix your color fun and creative action—and there you have it, your perfect day!

High for Life - The best case scenario!

 Day 47

HIGH-FOR-LIFE EQUALS FEELING LIFE DEEPLY, openheartedly, and to the smallest level of it all. Go sit with ants, seeds, and dust bunnies—feel what they are made of, the reason they are here, their energetic value, and what they are capable of in this life. What are you learning in these important meetings? What goodies do they bring to life? Remember, everything is the same energy, connected and shared at all times—meaning that everything that they are, you are too.

High for Life - The best case scenario!

ay 48

BEING high-for-life asks you to be a bit crazy and lose your mind, at least a little, in the process of living your life. From there, you can then think yourself and your life into amazingness without being stopped by old beliefs, untrue rules, or unfitting uptightness of how it's supposed to be. So think, think, and think again - higher than highest about yourself and about being alive - and go cook up some magic for yourself! Golden opportunities, being supernatural with no end, or being the luckiest person alive works well here. Go big, crazy journaler!

High for Life - The best case scenario!

 Day 49

LIVING high-for-life lets you smell your life - yes, you can actually smell it - in a vivid scent of glory and joy. What fragrance is your favorite? Write your scent list, even if it goes from flowery to barbecue-y, or to abundant whiffs of paper money. Be glamorous here! Now that you have your own aromatic orders for your perfect life, you obviously know exactly what to do.

High for Life - The best case scenario!

 ay 50

HEARING your life clearly and beyond what you can hear with your physical ears means you are living in a high-for-life frequency. Close your eyes - plug your ears too - and come up with a life that you love listening to by imagining the noises you love and prefer, then write about your favorite sounds. Is it your inner voice's loving guidance, your mind spinning into positivity, people's chitter-chatter, birds chirping loudly, your blood pumping through your veins, or a motorcycle's powerful *vroom-vroom*? That's your playlist to focus on—all else, let it go unheard!

High for Life - The best case scenario!

 Day 51

YOUR ONE-NESS with everything and everyone is a crucial ingredient to living high-for-life because it brings up the fact that everything you do, say, think, hear, feel, taste, smell, and create matters—since you always share yourself with everything and everyone. This also has the soothing essence of never being alone, but always connected and *ONE* with the whole world and beyond—a supported way of being and living. What will you choose differently, being so involved with everything? How will you show up as such a team-member?

High for Life - The best case scenario!

# Day 52

FALLING in love with all the individualism that is present in life means you are choosing to live life to the fullest and in your high-for-life frequency—even if not everything meets your preference. The colors, the wildly changing weather, the differences in nature, all the poles-apart type of people, millions of varieties of jobs and lifestyles, and the unique reasons of everyone - humans, animals, and all else - to be alive and here on Mother Earth, is the incredible diversity of physicality. What do you love about this crazy world of differences? How can you show up even more uniquely different? How can you be more *laissez fare* about everything and everyone?

_____
_____
_____
_____
_____
_____
_____
_____
_____
_____
_____
_____
_____
_____
_____
_____

High for Life - The best case scenario!

 Day 53

HIGH-FOR-LIFE PHYSICALITY IS BASED on an open-ness to understand, forgive, and move on—the lower scenario would be to stay weighted down. Many times that's easier said than done, however, you can get there anytime you choose. If the issue is small, understanding and moving on is appropriate—for instance when someone forgets a chore, understanding is of a higher essence than forgiving, because what's to forgive? If it's a bigger issue, collecting the understanding as a foundation and then forgiving is suitable. From there, moving on will be the natural thing to do. How open are you to such an enlightening practice? What and whom will you practice on?

High for Life - The best case scenario!

 ay 54

CHOOSING a chuckle over a frown wins every time! How will you chuckle ahead and not give in to groaning and moaning—even if the temptation is huge?

___

High for Life - The best case scenario!

 Day 55

HIGH-FOR-LIFE MEANS that you give up the need to do it all yourself. Instead, realize that everything is always a co-creation between your whole being and the Universe—and everyone else in-between. Give yourself a break by only taking on your part, which is being in alignment with who you really are. From that connection, do your actions in physical life with joy. For the rest, smile and with gratitude tell the Universe "I did my part, now it's your turn!" What tasks will you scoop onto your plate—and which ones are you serving the mighty Universe?

High for Life - The best case scenario!

 ay 56

Do you like tea? It's such a simple yet, profound thing in life because every cup is filled with loads of plentifulness. Energetically it represents peace, relaxation, deep breathing, and healing, while physically it is hydration and also good nutrition. In life, it creates time and a slow-down moment. What is your favorite tea? Are you interested in having a cup, or trying a new one? When is your high-for-life teatime happening?

___

High for Life - The best case scenario!

# Day 57

GOING for the minimum can give you the maximum! Eating minimal food at night lets you sleep tight—waking up fresh and clean the next morning. Minimal amounts of work or chores when it's time to slow down is key for good recovery or faster healing. Minimal amounts of giving, when your cup is empty, is key in order to level up your tank of high-for-life existing. So you see, aligned minimalism can be a very good thing. Where will you become a minimalist?

___

High for Life - The best case scenario!

Day 58

YESTERDAY'S TALK was all about minimalism, so let's give maximalism the focus today. *Maximum* has the energetic value of big, huge, powerful, strong, and opportunities. It also comes with the fact that once reached, a higher maximum is automatically created—showing an alignment with your high-for-life being that is always wanting to go higher and higher. What is a maximum for you—in anything, really? How do your different maximums in life look and feel like—are they even real, since there is never a ceiling to anything? Go on, get comfy with your maximums!

High for Life - The best case scenario!

 ay 59

Is it really true that you are stressing about a certain space in your place—one that is too dirty, too disorderly or cluttered, not freshly painted, simply too small, or not perfectly fitting right now? You have two high-for-life choices here. Either you change your perception about that space, or you make a change to a better fitting one—but stressing, that's far from feeling highly. Rather, it's a typical energy sucking habit. What is stressing you? What are your higher choices? Choose wisely, journaler!

High for Life - The best case scenario!

# Day 60

BEING grateful is an automatic and immediate jump into your own pool of happiness, and an invitation to swim in synchronicity with your deep purpose—just like putting on your bathing suit is a direct invitation to go make a splash. Why? Because gratitude is an action of your heart, which is the host of your inner being and naturally has the ceremonial flavor of love, light, and peace. How will you make a grateful splash—and how do you feel when in action?

_____
_____
_____
_____
_____
_____
_____
_____
_____
_____
_____
_____
_____
_____
_____
_____
_____
_____

High for Life - The best case scenario!

# Day 61

KNOWING and bragging about your fortes - remember, you have many - is of utmost value because it sets the tone of "I understand myself," "I have my own back," and "I support myself unconditionally." It also nourishes your self-pride and self-worth to the highest point possible—not to mention the true alignment you create with who you really are, by taking full responsibility of how you feel. Bragging accomplishes a lot! So here we go, your brag-sheet please!

_____
_____
_____
_____
_____
_____
_____
_____
_____
_____
_____
_____
_____
_____
_____
_____
_____
_____

High for Life - The best case scenario!

ay 62

BEING and living high-for-life lets you slide into a state of "I am me" and "they are they," leaving only the question: ***What and who am I even when they are they?*** Are you shifting with your surroundings, or are you staying put in your alignment of being and living your high-for-life ways? The latter is obviously the better one here. How will you stay yourself in the one-ness with the world more often? How will you let them be them—while you are staying you?

___
___
___
___
___
___
___
___
___
___
___
___
___
___
___
___
___
___

High for Life - The best case scenario!

 Day 63

HIGH-FOR-LIFE BEING and living means you always put a little more umpf on top of how you're experiencing life right now—like animating a movie and turning up the volume. When you talk, talk with more energy in your words. When walking, put a fun skip into every step—when you eat, "hmmm" and "ahhhh" about your food with energized vocalization. When smiling, have an undeniable upward curve—and when you sing, strut those vocals no matter how it sounds! Be louder, crazier, and much more colorful, or pretend to be in a broadway show entertaining the audience and yourself. What do you say?

High for Life - The best case scenario!

Day 64

RECYCLING—TO use what's there and not waste a thing. Do that with what's in your life! Look around and focus on what makes you happy, smile, or gives you a giggle—tap into that energy and fill every single cell of your whole being while consciously shifting into your higher-for-life frequency. Once done, look around again to find what makes you happy now that you are feeling higher—recycle again by tapping into this blissful energy, filling yourself to the brim, and mindfully noticing your higher shift. On and on you go, you recycler!

High for Life - The best case scenario!

 ay 65

IN A HIGH-FOR-LIFE PHYSICALITY, you follow your heart's instinct and move the way it fits for you. Choosing a few exercise modalities that you like, then asking, "Which one feels amazing today, or right now?" is key in creating a healthy exercise habit, aside from moving in alignment with who you are. Some days that means your movement will be slower, while on others, it will be rigorous; but most importantly, it means that you are moving with the flow of your ever-changing you. What exercise styles do you enjoy? How will you make sure to enjoy at least one once a day—making yourself a priority once a day?

High for Life - The best case scenario!

 ay 66

WHAT ARE YOUR BLISS WORDS? What sentences shoot you into a high-for-life frequency? What sayings make your heart skip with joy? Maybe statements like: "Everything is always possible!" "Life loves me!" "I'm always supported!" "I love myself!" Make your tool-box of magical words—then say, think, and feel them often!

High for Life - The best case scenario!

Day 67

ARE YOU DREAMING ENOUGH? Could you dream even more? Will you dream higher, then even higher, for yourself and your life? Please tell me you are into that sort of thing! Dream, journaler, dream—of your best life ever!

High for Life - The best case scenario!

Day 68

HIGH-FOR-LIFE IS ACCOMPLISHED when you give gas at the right time and hit the brakes when needed—refuel when empty, run on clean fuel, and do something when things are not working smoothly. Where and when will you take better care of yourself? Where can you give more gas, and when is it better to hit the breaks? What is clean fuel for you? How do you know when you are running empty? What are your go-to tricks when things are uneasy—is it meditation, pampering, sleep, or rest?

___

High for Life - The best case scenario!

Day 69

WHEN WAS the last time you yawned really good and big, laughed out so loud it made people jump, skipped down the road feeling young and playful, were enjoying your food vividly, started to dance without giving a warning, sang a happy "thank you" to someone in the store, or tossed a bag of marshmallows at your shopping partner—just for them to catch it in surprise? Oh c'mon, when? What silly-billy stuff can you cook up to make today your chuckle day?

_____
_____
_____
_____
_____
_____
_____
_____
_____
_____
_____
_____
_____
_____
_____
_____
_____
_____

High for Life - The best case scenario!

 ay 70

THERE IS *MORE* IN EVERYTHING—FIND that *more*, focus on it, and fill yourself with this *more*. You are *more* than just your physical body—you are also a mind, a soul being, and consciousness. There is *more* to life than living it solely through your physicality—there is a whole energetic essence that is you, here to expand and calibrate into a higher you at all times. There is *more* to every physical symptom—a whole bag of wisdom sits underneath the surface. Everything in your awareness is always spiked with *more* than you can see, hear, taste, smell, think, and feel as your human you, and it's all there waiting for you. What *more* can you find? What *more* will you look into?

High for Life - The best case scenario!

 Day 71

Do you remember as a child imagining the coolest things when playing, running around, crafting, or looking at books? Which ones made you feel happy? What was the story behind them—being a pirate, a parent, or a teacher? What was the setting; did you play alone or with friends? What was the outcome—a wonderful time? Now that you have shifted into your childlike playfulness, what imaginations today as your now YOU make you happy? What is the story behind them, and what is the setting? What's the outcome—a blissful time? Be really imaginative here!

___

High for Life - The best case scenario!

 Day 72

ALLOWING and receiving are both important behaviors in living the life of your dreams and in being high-for-life. What are you allowing, and are you allowing enough of it? What will you allow more? Are you openly receiving, and if so, what are you freely receiving? What will you receive more of? Make your gift list!

High for Life - The best case scenario!

Day 73

LIVING LIMITLESSLY IS VERY POWERFUL, and an immediate shift into a high-for-life frequency—aside from *that* being your energetic truth. Are you living the way that you are living because you believe that you are limited? Would you do what you do, and also keep doing it the way that you are doing it, with the knowledge that you are limitless? What in your life will you do differently, now that you know of your limitlessness on the energetic level? I say, spread your wings and fly!

High for Life - The best case scenario!

# Day 74

HIGH-FOR-LIFE MEANS that you are YOU! It also means that you take 100% responsibility for yourself. How will you stay in your lane of purity without getting too mixed up with the masses? How can you align with your inner being and stay unshakable? How will you create a life that fits your own unique personality? Is it by making your quality of life your duty?

___

High for Life - The best case scenario!

 Day 75

BREATHE, journaler, breathe! First thing you did when coming into the light of Mother Earth was breathe—so why is focusing on this life-saving action so hard? Why is it that something so special gets forgotten more often than not—especially when you are in distress? You guessed it! It's because it's automatic and goes on no matter if you notice, nourish, or care about it—but it's doing exactly those things in life that make everything so special. I say, no more of that nonsense; instead, celebrate your breathing consciously! How will you honor that high-for-life happening of yours?

High for Life - The best case scenario!

 ay 76

EVERYTHING IS ALWAYS A GIFT! That is THE mantra for being and living high-for-life, and is absolutely true since everything always has two sides. What is really really hard, or even unbearable, in your life right now? Make your rampage list! Next, take that list and find the high-for-life version from that angle. For example, a headache communicates better self-care; a job loss opens up new possibilities; a fight strengthens your character. The mess-ups are usually gifts in disguise. Go on, brave one!

___

High for Life - The best case scenario!

 Day 77

Showing up without feeling the need or pressure to be more proper, more valuable, or totally different is the equivalent of high-for-life. Of course running naked through the streets is not what I mean here, since it might not be legal and neither is seriously hurting someone. It's showing up as the best version of you that you can be while not budging an inch that I am talking about, because that is your birthright. What kind of high-for-life being, character, personality, energy are you really? How do you feel as such a truthful you? How can you show your clearly aligned YOU more often?

High for Life - The best case scenario!

 Day 78

HIGH-FOR-LIFE LIVING means that you let go of what does not serve you anymore—no matter how much you once loved it, how beautiful it still is, and certainly not minding if others think you have lost your mind. Sure, be certain that it's not for you anymore by trying different scenarios to make it work, but when it is clear as water, make space for the better feeling next. What in your life - small or big - is the one to let go of, and is clear as can be?

___

High for Life - The best case scenario!

Day 79

HIGH-FOR-LIFE MEANS that you stick with a fitting balance between making it right for you, and giving help to others. If you put yourself below someone else's needs you will either need to find a way to support them while still making it right for you, or change your perception of the support you are giving by focusing on your nice deed, the joy of the helped one, or that they need it more than you right now. If neither of those are possible, then your act of helping is of a lower energy for yourself and others. In that case, making it right for you by sticking with your alignment of "me first" is the better plan. Where are you helping without it being fitting for you? How could you change that—or would letting go of the old habit, of putting yourself always last, be an option?

High for Life - The best case scenario!

Day 80

LIVING *all* of you in *all* of life—fitting and aligned with your inner being and every occasion you encounter, is the wonderful buffet available for you to chose from anew and anew. So it's good to be a strong force ready to fight for the better, but life also invites you to be snuggly as a kitten when that's the perfect way to be. How are you going to keep up with the constant shifting and turning of being YOU? Would a clarifying, high-for-life chit-chat with your inner being do?

High for Life - The best case scenario!

 ay 81

Passions are wonderful feeling activities, but even more importantly, they are your direct alignment with your inner being—hence, your passions take over. Passions also change all the time because you change, and so does life. How do you know if your passions have changed? When they start to feel like chores, a must, or are not exciting anymore, it's time to have a passion-talk with yourself. On the physical life level that change might look like you are a giver-upper, but energetically it means that you have expanded and calibrated into a higher you—wanting a higher aligned passion. What passions are you hanging onto like they're the only ones out there—and what newness gets you high-for-life?

_____
_____
_____
_____
_____
_____
_____
_____
_____
_____
_____
_____
_____
_____
_____

High for Life - The best case scenario!

ay 82

SIT in a place of stillness where there's no music, no noise, nothing. Feel the wideness and expansion in that experience until you can hear the open space of limitlessness. That is where everything is possible—where you can take deep breaths and can relax, so much so that you forget your name or where you came from. Feel yourself widening beyond your physical outline and sense what's possible in that sacred space of nothingness. How does this feel for you? Can you sense your deep love for yourself and for life in that pure spot? Which place - in your home or out in nature - will you choose to practice such a high-for-life connection to yourself and to consciousness?

___

High for Life - The best case scenario!

Day 83

POCKETS of inner peace and harmony are split seconds that are filled with wonder and awe. They are created by you floating in the beauty of "I don't care," "I don't know," "whatever," "whoever," and "whenever"—with the amazing outcome of glorious realizations and aha-moments. When was the last time you let yourself go there? It's time, journaler! How, and when, will you give yourself permission to do so?

High for Life - The best case scenario!

 Day 84

FEELING high-for-life includes your interest in your physical body—and the depth of your physical pains, symptoms, or issues. Why? Because there lie your clues! For instance, asking your back pain what in your life is breaking your back, has enormous value. So does asking your headache about what in your life is worth such pain, a sore throat about where you are not speaking up, and your intestines about what in life is hard to digest—or your painful feet that tell you all about the unfitting journeying you are doing. Make your pain-list here and own the wisdom that is yours!

_____
_____
_____
_____
_____
_____
_____
_____
_____
_____
_____
_____
_____
_____
_____
_____
_____
_____

High for Life - The best case scenario!

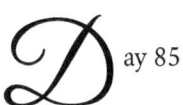 Day 85

YOU ARE A BIG ENERGY! Think of your anger and how much power that incredible force is. Feel yourself into happy—sense how you shift the whole world as that bliss. Take your huge love and all of the hearts you touch that way, but also be aware of your great downer energy and how it can bring the whole house to its knees—everyone has it! You are huge! How will you tap into your bigness and show up as such unapologetically? Uplifting is preferred here!

High for Life - The best case scenario!

Day 86

WHAT'S the craziest thing you have ever done? How did you feel when doing it? Why is it *the one* experience in your life—what made it so super special? What did it take for you to say yes to it —to plan and create it? Was it hard to be that crazy? How long did the phenomenal feeling last? Are you still talking or thinking about it to this day? Now that you got such clarity, how can you go for more of these crazy things in your life? What could be of such value, to feel like that—and how can you milk it to no end?

High for Life - The best case scenario!

 Day 87

ABRACADABRA! If you would have a magic wand, what would you change, want, shift, create, desire, or do in your life to feel high-for-life right now? List please, and get real candid with yourself! Then realize that you actually do have such a magic tool - your inner light - and that once aligned, you also ARE that magic wand—yours to use and to become without any remorse. Go be a shiner and use your shiner abilities! FYI, shiner people are the ones that shine their light bright no matter what.

High for Life - The best case scenario!

 ay 88

WHAT'S YOUR HAPPY PLACE? How does it look, feel, and sound? What's included and what's not? Is there any invited drama—or is it a drama free zone? Are there old gunky rules in your joy world? What will you keep pumping into your newly gained playspace—perhaps love, abundance, and bliss? Go all high-for-life here!

High for Life - The best case scenario!

ay 89

ON SOME DAYS - or in some split seconds - feeling phenomenally aligned means you are a hermit, and barely move. Question is, are you hermit-ing because it is in alignment for you, or because of something else—like not wanting to face the world, which is not in alignment? How will you go along with your well-feeling desires and either allow yourself to rest, or push yourself out of the house since even a hermit needs outside action to stay aligned? And how will you let everyone around you know that an aligned hermit life is OK—allowing yourself to be still for as long as needed?

High for Life - The best case scenario!

 ay 90

STEPPING into a powerful co-creational relationship with the Universe in which you take full responsibility for your physicality - your actions, focus, feelings, way of living, and doings - while giving the Universe the benefit of the doubt that it has your back, loves you immensely, and presents you always with everything that's FOR you - never to or against you - means that you are teaming up with THE force. How much better can that get? How does such a high-for-life relationship look and feel like to you—and how will you go everywhere as such?

_____
_____
_____
_____
_____
_____
_____
_____
_____
_____
_____
_____

High for Life - The best case scenario!

* * *

Ready to continue on your self-growth path? Get the next journal in this series: ***Bragging: Because you're worth it!***

BONUS

Because hey, nobody ever wants the goodness to end.

Keep on high-for-life-ing because there is never a ceiling!

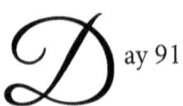 ay 91

PICK ONE HIGH-FOR-LIFE THOUGHT, emotion, feeling, activity, act, word, color, treat, scent, view, taste, and happening—small or big does not matter here. List one, or even better, many, then breathe into these high-for-life scenarios, and focus on them for the next 7 days by making them your well-feeling tools—of course, while continuing with a page a day in this journal. After the week is through, come back, and realize how great you feel, and start your next weekly plan while journaling page by page.

High for Life - The best case scenario!

 ay 92

CHOOSE one concrete high-for-life essence in nature that shifts you immediately into your higher-than-high place. What is it— an animal, a flower or plant, fruits or vegetables, the sky, the sun, the moon, or the stars, the ocean? Pick a few if that's your jam! How do they make you feel? How will you use these nature-tools as great shifters? Would a T-Shirt with pineapples do—if pineapples are the ones? Or some beach printed socks?

_____
_____
_____
_____
_____
_____
_____
_____
_____
_____
_____
_____
_____
_____
_____
_____
_____
_____
_____

High for Life - The best case scenario!

ay 93

HIGH-FOR-LIFE MEANS KNOWING that you always have unlimited time to stop and smile, laugh, be happy, enjoy, or do nothing else other than being blissful. It takes time to be joyous, just like it takes time to cook, clean, shop, or do your work—so give yourself that time! How will you schedule *happiness* on your day-to-day calendar?

High for Life - The best case scenario!

 ay 94

NAY-SAYERS, negative-ers, and down-ers! In truth, they are still in their high-for-life frequency - even if it does not look like that from your point of view - because their low could be even lower, making how they are behaving their high-for-life way of being for right now. You are expanding on your own terms and through journaling here you have calibrated into an even higher self—making them seem even lower to you. Great news is that you never have to match where anybody is. Instead, you can keep climbing higher and higher at your own pace while perceiving them being at their highest point possible—shifting them into a higher value for you while sharing that higher energy with them. This way, everyone wins!

High for Life - The best case scenario!

# Day 95

WHAT CHOICES from your past would you not renew anymore, yet still are living? List them without judgment because not only is judging a lower value, but the past is also the past, and you chose what felt best for you back then. There is no need to dig deep into your old decisions or the *what* and *why*. Instead, and with pride say, "I choose new, again, to give myself the best NOW!" Choosing as your power of freedom while flying high-for-life, what newness will you decide for yourself?

High for Life - The best case scenario!

AND NOW IT'S YOUR TURN!

The following are your magical pages to keep cracking your illusionary ceiling of limits!

I'm counting on you to go high-for-life here!

Day 96

HIGH-FOR-LIFE MEANS...

High for Life - The best case scenario!

Day 97

HIGH-FOR-LIFE MEANS...

High for Life - The best case scenario!

# Day 98

HIGH-FOR-LIFE MEANS...

High for Life - The best case scenario!

 ay 99

High-for-life means...

High for Life - The best case scenario!

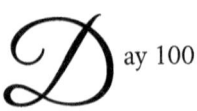 ay 100

HIGH-FOR-LIFE MEANS...

_____
_____
_____
_____
_____
_____
_____
_____
_____
_____
_____
_____
_____
_____
_____
_____
_____
_____
_____

High for Life - The best case scenario!

* * *

Don't forget to leave a review on Amazon.com and Goodreads.com as soon as you can, as your kind feedback helps other readers find my books easier. Thank you!

ALSO BY JACQUELINE PIRTLE

365 Days of Happiness

Because happiness is a piece of cake!

This passage book invites you to create a daily habit to live your every day joy, and is the parent companion to *365 Days of Happiness*, the journal workbook.

* * *

365 Days of Happiness - Special Edition

Because happiness is a piece of cake

This beautiful Special Edition of the bestseller *365 Days of Happiness: Because happiness is a piece of cake* has room for your notes after every daily passage.

* * *

365 Days of Happiness - Journal Workbook

Because happiness is a piece of cake

This enlightening journal workbook is your daily tool to create a habit of living your every day bliss, and is the companion to *365 Days of Happiness: Because happiness is a piece of cake*.

* * *

Life IS Beautiful - Here's to New Beginnings

If you like digging deeper into the meaning of life and are inspired by spirituality, then you'll love Jacqueline's effective teachings.

* * *

Parenting Through the Eyes of Lollipops

A Guide to Conscious Parenting

If you like harmony at home and laughter in the house, then you'll love Jacqueline's inspirational methods.

What it Means to BE a Woman

And Yes! Women do Poop!

If you like to live free, empowered, and want to decide for yourself, then you'll love Jacqueline's liberating ways.

What. If. - Turning your what IFs into it IS!

A 30 Day or 90 Day - Extended Edition - Journal

If you like to be in charge of your own life, turn your dreams into reality, and enjoy journaling then you'll love Jacqueline's uplifting teachings.

Open - Where it all starts!

A 30 Day or 90 Day - Extended Edition - Journal

If you like to be open to live your life fully, allow your dreams to come true, and enjoy journaling then you'll love Jacqueline's uplifting teachings.

To BE and Live - The reason you are here!

A 30 Day or 90 Day - Extended Edition - Journal

If you like to feel alive, wish for your dreams to come true, and enjoy journaling, then you'll love Jacqueline's levitating teachings.

ABOUT THE AUTHOR

Bestselling author, podcaster, and holistic practitioner, Jacqueline Pirtle, has twenty-four years of experience helping thousands of clients discover their own happiness. Jacqueline is the owner of *FreakyHealer* and has shared her solid teachings through her podcast *The Daily Freak*, sessions, workshops, presentations, and books with clients all over the world. She holds international degrees in holistic health and natural living. Her effective healing work has been featured in print and online magazines, podcasts, radio shows, on TV, and in the documentary *The Overly Emotional Child by Learning Success*, available on Amazon Prime.

For any questions you might have, to sign up for Jacqueline's newsletter, and for more information on whatever else she is up to, visit www.freakyhealer.com and her social media accounts @freakyhealer.

www.ingramcontent.com/pod-product-compliance
Lightning Source LLC
LaVergne TN
LVHW012114070526
838202LV00056B/5735